THE BEST STORY AND WRITING PROMPT JOURNAL EVER!!

STORY PROMPTS,

BRAINSTORMING EXERCISES,

AND PREWRITING TECHNIQUES TO

INSPIRE YOUNG CREATIVE WRITERS

GRADES 5–6

BY ORDER OF

The Mayor of Grammaropolis

Written by Christopher Knight
Interior Design by Christopher Knight
Cover Design by Mckee Frazior
Grammaropolis Character Design by Powerhouse Animation & Mckee Frazior

ISBN: 9781644420515
Copyright © 2021 by Grammaropolis LLC
All rights reserved.
Published by Six Foot Press
Printed in the U.S.A.

Grammaropolis.com
SixFootPress.com

THE BEST
STORY
AND WRITING
PROMPT JOURNAL
EVER!!

STORY PROMPTS,
BRAINSTORMING EXERCISES,
AND PREWRITING TECHNIQUES TO
INSPIRE YOUNG CREATIVE WRITERS
GRADES 5-6

GRAMMAROPOLIS BOOKS
HOUSTON

FROM THE DESK OF THE MAYOR

Greetings, fellow writer!

I want to congratulate you on picking up my story and writing prompt journal. I do think you'll find that it is indeed the best one ever. (If I do say so myself.)

Why is that, you may ask? Because this journal actually gives you space to prepare your thoughts with prewriting exercises *before* you start writing!

I know, I know. Prewriting and organizing and all that "preparation" stuff just feels like extra work. You don't want to do any more work than you already have to. But I'm here to tell you a secret: prewriting actually *saves* you time overall!

That's because the first idea that comes to mind isn't always the best one. If you give other ideas the chance to make it to the page, you may just be shocked by your own creativity!

Thanks again for visiting Grammaropolis. I hope you enjoy your stay!

–The Mayor

Table of Contents

Writing (Cont'd)

The Purposes of Writing

The first question to ask when you sit down to write something is simple: **Why am I writing this?** ("Because my teacher told me to" doesn't count!)

In other words, What is the **purpose** of this piece of writing?

To Inform

Informative writing is used to share facts and information about a topic. Factual information is the focus of informative writing; opinions and appeals to emotion are to be avoided.

To Explain

Similar in many ways to informative writing, explanatory writing seeks to tell **how** or **why** about a particular topic. For example, you would use explanatory writing to tell how something is made.

To Persuade

The goal of persuasive writing is to express an opinion or a position in order to persuade others. It's extremely important to include facts, reasons, and other information to support your position.

To Describe

The main goal of descriptive writing is to use sensory details to describe a person, place, or thing. Descriptive writing can add depth and detail to other purposes as well.

To Entertain

Poetry, fiction, and personal narrative are all examples of writing to entertain. Narrative elements may include setting, characterization, dialogue, and story structure (beginning, middle, end).

Once you determine the purpose of your writing, the rest of the writing process will fall into place.

Prewriting

Prewriting Techniques

If you need to get unstuck, to build on something you're already thinking about, or just to get as many ideas onto the page as possible, here are some prewriting techniques you may find useful.

Freewrite

A freewrite is essentially a stream of consciousness. Go wherever your brain wants you to go!

Brainstorm

Similar to a freewrite, a brainstorm is a way to get ideas on the page without worrying about whether you'll end up using them.

Cluster

A type of organized brainstorm, a cluster will help you gather your ideas into categories.

5W & H

Asking *Who, What, When, Where, Why,* and *How* is a great way to develop a lot of information about a topic.

Venn Diagram

Another type of organized brainstorm, the Venn diagram is particularly useful when you need to compare and contrast.

Five Senses

Information developed with your five senses is wonderful for generating material for descriptive writing.

Series of Events

Before you start to tell a story, it can be helpful to list the things that happened so that you don't forget any important parts.

Character Sketch

Spending some time thinking about your characters is a great way to develop your story and to make it more interesting.

Prewriting Technique Examples

Prewriting may seem like extra work, but even a little bit of time spent before starting to write will make a huge difference.

Let's do some prewriting with each of the techniques for the same writing prompt.

Think of the time when you felt most proud of yourself. Why were you so proud? What happened?

Remember, the prewriting techniques are:

Freewrite

Brainstorm

Cluster

5W & H

Venn Diagram

Five Senses

Series of Events

Character Sketch

Pay particular attention to the different types of information that you can generate with each prewriting technique!

Prewriting Technique: Freewrite

This is one of the most basic prewriting techniques there is. You simply put pen to paper and see where your brain takes you! A freewrite is useful when you don't know what you want to talk about and need to generate potential ideas.

There have only been a couple of times when I have been so proud that I actually patted myself on my own back. Some people think that being proud of yourself is bragging, but other people say that it's not bragging if it's true, so maybe it's okay for me to literally pat myself on the back. I was at my friend Garvin's house and Garvin's mom and dad are both really good cooks so whenever I go to their house I know that I am going to get awesome food. Garvin wanted to do something nice for his parents because it was their anniversary but he didn't know how to cook, so he asked me to help him. I know a little bit about how to cook because my cousin Sara used to let me help her make breakfast. But Garvin and I never cooked together before. We did lots of other stuff together though, like riding bikes and playing video games and playing in the park with my dog Stella. Stella is a yellow labrador and she is the cutest thing in the world. Sometimes she sleeps with me in my bed even though I'm supposed to make her sleep on the floor. But she is so cute that I can't ever do that. My dad once said that I love Stella so much because she doesn't make me clean my room, and I think he might have a point. Another time I was proud of myself was when I cleaned my room without my dad telling me to do it, and he came in and gave me a high five.

Prewriting Technique: Brainstorm

If it pops into your head, it goes on the page. You may not actually use most of what you generate, but that's okay! The *storm* is what's important. Like a freewrite, a brainstorm is helpful for prewriting any of the purposes.

Dinner for Garvin's parents
Showed Garvin how to fry an egg.
Garvin's parents anniversary
Eggs for dinner
Actually patted myself on the back!

Taught myself how to do a handstand
Fell on my head the first couple of times

Gave my sister my coat when it was cold
Surprised my sister AND my mom!
I was cold
Felt good for some reason anyway
Almost made fun of her for forgetting her coat

Memorized my home address when I was six

Got a 100 on a math test
Ususally not great at math
Didn't feel like studying but made myself do it
Went out for ice cream after
Not scared of teacher anymore
Studied for a whole hour the day before

Broke the school record in the long jump even though I didn't know I was even going to do the long jump

Prewriting Technique: Cluster

To brainstorm with a little bit of structure, a cluster will help show the relationships between your ideas. You can also see what might need to be developed a bit more. A cluster can be useful for any purpose.

Prewriting Technique: 5W & H

Otherwise known as the "Journalist's Questions," 5W & H is a way not only to generate information that you already know but also to help determine what you need to find out. This technique is ideal for informative or explanatory writing.

WHO?

My friend, Garvin
His parents, Mr. & Mrs. James
Me

WHAT?

Dinner of fried eggs, mashed potatoes, diet soda, fresh green beans, fresh carrots, fresh snap peas, hummus.

WHERE?

Garvin's house. In the kitchen, mostly. With some time spent in the back yard while the potatoes boiled and then some time in the dining room while we ate.

WHEN?

About six months ago. In the evening. On a Saturday, April 27. After Garvin's soccer game when he scored a goal on a penalty kick

WHY?

Garvin's parents have always been nice to me, and I knew it was their anniversary, so I told Garvin that we would earn big-time brownie points if we cooked for them.

HOW?

We walked to the store and bought eggs and potatoes and hummus with Garvin's savings, and then we boiled the potatoes before mashing and I taught Garvin to fry eggs.

Prewriting Technique: Venn Diagram

A Venn diagram is a type of structured brainstorm that shows you what the similarities and differences are between two subjects. This is particularly useful if the purpose of your writing is to compare and contrast.

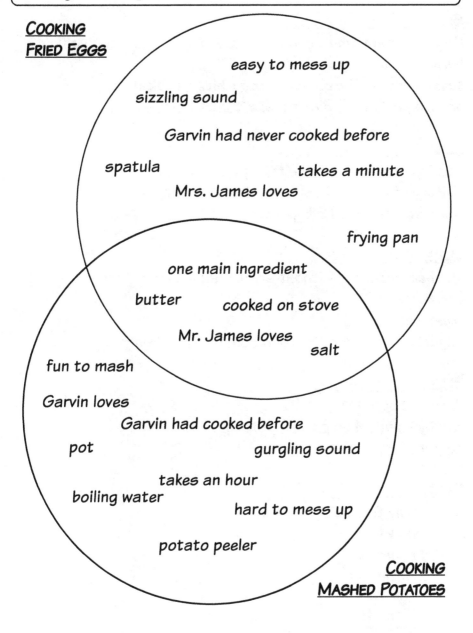

COOKING
FRIED EGGS

easy to mess up

sizzling sound

Garvin had never cooked before

spatula

takes a minute

Mrs. James loves

frying pan

one main ingredient

butter

cooked on stove

Mr. James loves

salt

fun to mash

Garvin loves

Garvin had cooked before

pot

gurgling sound

takes an hour

boiling water

hard to mess up

potato peeler

COOKING
MASHED POTATOES

Prewriting Technique: Five Senses

Using your five senses is a great way to develop descriptive information and details. Whether your purpose is to describe or to tell a story, prewriting with your five senses will generate details that help the reader connect to your writing.

SEE

Bright kitchen, white countertop, 4-burner stove with all burners going.
total mess on the counter- egg whites, broken yolk, some potato peels that didn't make it into the trash.

HEAR

sizzling of the egg in the frying pan
clinking of potato masher against the pot
bubbling sound of boiling water

TASTE

Mashed potatoes without enough salt. Bland. Then more salt and butter!
Fresh carrots.
Slightly burnt edges of fried egg. Buttery. Egg yolk.

SMELL

Burning butter
Earthy scent when peeling potatoes
Pepper in my nose

TOUCH

Hot handle for the frying pan
Slimy egg white
Gooey hummus
Cold countertop

Prewriting Technique: Series of Events

You may think you remember all of the events in a story you want to tell (or all of the steps in a process you want to explain) but prewriting is helpful to make sure you haven't forgotten anything important and that your events are in the right order.

I went to Garvin's house after school

We decided to do something special for Garvin's parents

We spent ten minutes trying to find a potato peeler in the store

We rode our bikes to the store

We surprised Garvin's parents with an announcement that we were cooking dinner for them

Garvin squeezed the egg too hard when he was trying to crack it and the egg white went everywhere

Garvin admitted that he had never fried an egg

I peeled the potatoes and almost cut a big chunk out of my finger

Garvin started calling them "finger potatoes"

I turned the stove up too high and burned the butter, and smoke filled the kitchen

Garvin's dad asked if I wanted him to call the fire department

Garvin finally figured out how to crack an egg without getting it everywhere

Mr. & Mrs. James ate everything we served them!

I was super proud

I put all the food on a plate and took it to the dining room

Prewriting Technique: Character Sketch

To make your story more vibrant, whether it's a piece of fiction or a personal narrative, try brainstorming details about your characters. Even if your final draft doesn't include all the details you generate, your characters will still feel more real.

GARVIN

has been my best friend since we were three years old

loves chocolate and cheeseburgers, in that order

short, curly hair and brown eyes

three inches taller than me

wants to be a professional basketball, but is a much better singer than a basketball player

once tripped on the curb and knocked his front teeth

has a huge collection of Pokemon cards that he never actually looks at

goofy

gets super angry when you eat his dessert when he isn't looking

absolutely loves to play practical jokes on people. One time he cooked some spaghetti and replaced the laces in his dad's running shoes with the cooked spaghetti, and then when the spaghetti dried, it got all crispy and looked hilarous!

really good at math

like, REALLY good at math, even though he hardly ever studies, which drives everyone else in class crazy

has a birthmark behind his left ear

Writing

Writing Exercises

For each exercise, you'll have the choice between two different writing prompts.

1. Choose one of the prompts to write about.

2. Decide what purpose you're going to use.
Now you already know what you're going to be writing about and what the goal of your writing is going to be. That's a lot!

3. Choose a prewriting technique.
As you're making your choice here, don't forget about your purpose. Some prewriting techniques are better suited to some purposes than others.

4. Prewrite.
There are no bad ideas when you're prewriting, but remember that the first thing that comes to mind isn't always going to be the best or most interesting one.

You can also do more than one prewriting exercise for a single prompt. You might do a freewrite just to get some ideas on the page. From there, you might choose one of the ideas from your freewrite and then use it as the starting point for a brainstorm or cluster.

5. Examine the results of your prewriting.
You didn't prewrite just for the sake of prewriting. You did it to generate ideas for your writing. So take a moment to look at what you came up with. Add to it. Circle stuff. Cross things out. Draw arrows from one idea to another. Make your prewriting count for something!

6. Write.
Now you're ready to build on your ideas from the prewriting technique. It's go time!

Writing Exercise #1

1. Underline your choice of prompt:
   a. What is the bravest thing you have ever done for someone?
   b. Dancing pineapple

2. Determine a purpose for your writing: _____

3. Select an appropriate prewriting exercise: _____

4. Use the next two pages for prewriting!

Take a moment to select and organize (and even add to) the parts of your prewriting that you feel best support your purpose.

Now it's time to write. Remember that you can use the prewriting work on these pages as a guide, but if you feel inspired to go in a different direction while you're writing, go for it!

Story Title:

Writing Exercise #2

1. Underline your choice of prompt:
   a. Would you rather live on the Moon or on Mars?
   b. Start a story with this line: *I swear I didn't do it!*

2. Determine a purpose for your writing: _____

3. Select an appropriate prewriting exercise: _____

4. Use the next two pages for prewriting!

Take a moment to select and organize (and even add to) the parts of your prewriting that you feel best support your purpose.

Now it's time to write. Remember that you can use the prewriting work on these pages as a guide, but if you feel inspired to go in a different direction while you're writing, go for it!

Story Title:

_____

Writing Exercise #3

1. Underline your choice of prompt:
   a. **Write a story that takes place on your teacher's birthday.**
   b. **Would you rather never drink carbonated drinks again or *only* drink carbonated drinks for the rest of your life?**

2. Determine a purpose for your writing: _____

3. Select an appropriate prewriting exercise: _____

4. Use the next two pages for prewriting!

Take a moment to select and organize (and even add to) the parts of your prewriting that you feel best support your purpose.

Now it's time to write. Remember that you can use the prewriting work on these pages as a guide, but if you feel inspired to go in a different direction while you're writing, go for it!

Story Title:

Writing Exercise #4

1. Underline your choice of prompt:
   a. **Start a story with this line:** *It was a difficult question to answer.*
   b. **Artistic freedom with crayons**

2. Determine a purpose for your writing: _____

3. Select an appropriate prewriting exercise: _____

4. Use the next two pages for prewriting!

Take a moment to select and organize (and even add to) the parts of your prewriting that you feel best support your purpose.

Now it's time to write. Remember that you can use the prewriting work on these pages as a guide, but if you feel inspired to go in a different direction while you're writing, go for it!

Story Title:

Writing Exercise #5

1. Underline your choice of prompt:
   a. Spaghetti house
   b. Would you rather receive bad news in person or over the phone? How about good news? Why?

2. Determine a purpose for your writing: _____

3. Select an appropriate prewriting exercise: _____

4. Use the next two pages for prewriting!

Take a moment to select and organize (and even add to) the parts of your prewriting that you feel best support your purpose.

Now it's time to write. Remember that you can use the prewriting work on these pages as a guide, but if you feel inspired to go in a different direction while you're writing, go for it!

Story Title:

Writing Exercise #6

1. Underline your choice of prompt:
   a. **Start a story with this line:** *I had never seen so much chocolate in my life.*
   b. **What is one thing you really regret?**

2. Determine a purpose for your writing: _____

3. Select an appropriate prewriting exercise: _____

4. Use the next two pages for prewriting!

Take a moment to select and organize (and even add to) the parts of your prewriting that you feel best support your purpose.

Now it's time to write. Remember that you can use the prewriting work on these pages as a guide, but if you feel inspired to go in a different direction while you're writing, go for it!

Story Title:

Writing Exercise #7

1. Underline your choice of prompt:
   a. **Flowering banana tree**
   b. **If you could be invisible (but only for one hour), what would you do with that hour?**

2. Determine a purpose for your writing: _____

3. Select an appropriate prewriting exercise: _____

4. Use the next two pages for prewriting!

Take a moment to select and organize (and even add to) the parts of your prewriting that you feel best support your purpose.

Now it's time to write. Remember that you can use the prewriting work on these pages as a guide, but if you feel inspired to go in a different direction while you're writing, go for it!

Story Title:

Writing Exercise #8

1. Underline your choice of prompt:
   a. What is your favorite condiment and why?
   b. What is one habit you'd like to develop?

2. Determine a purpose for your writing: _____

3. Select an appropriate prewriting exercise: _____

4. Use the next two pages for prewriting!

Take a moment to select and organize (and even add to) the parts of your prewriting that you feel best support your purpose.

Now it's time to write. Remember that you can use the prewriting work on these pages as a guide, but if you feel inspired to go in a different direction while you're writing, go for it!

Story Title:

_____

Writing Exercise #9

1. Underline your choice of prompt:

    a. Start a story with this line: *The last thing I remember was Franklin's enormous tooth coming right at me.*

    b. What will your day look like exactly 10 years from today?

2. Determine a purpose for your writing: _____

3. Select an appropriate prewriting exercise: _____

4. Use the next two pages for prewriting!

Take a moment to select and organize (and even add to) the parts of your prewriting that you feel best support your purpose.

Now it's time to write. Remember that you can use the prewriting work on these pages as a guide, but if you feel inspired to go in a different direction while you're writing, go for it!

Story Title:

Writing Exercise #10

1. Underline your choice of prompt:
   a. How are you similar to your family? How are you different?
   b. Invisible dry-erase markers

2. Determine a purpose for your writing: _____

3. Select an appropriate prewriting exercise: _____

4. Use the next two pages for prewriting!

Take a moment to select and organize (and even add to) the parts of your prewriting that you feel best support your purpose.

Now it's time to write. Remember that you can use the prewriting work on these pages as a guide, but if you feel inspired to go in a different direction while you're writing, go for it!

Story Title:

Writing Exercise #11

1. Underline your choice of prompt:

   a. **Would you rather have lots of good friends or one great friend?**

   b. **Start a story with this line:** ***It was a total walrus symphony.***

2. Determine a purpose for your writing: _____

3. Select an appropriate prewriting exercise: _____

4. Use the next two pages for prewriting!

Take a moment to select and organize (and even add to) the parts of your prewriting that you feel best support your purpose.

Now it's time to write. Remember that you can use the prewriting work on these pages as a guide, but if you feel inspired to go in a different direction while you're writing, go for it!

Story Title:

_____

Writing Exercise #12

1. Underline your choice of prompt:
   a. A bag full of spatulas
   b. When was a time that you felt bullied?

2. Determine a purpose for your writing: _____

3. Select an appropriate prewriting exercise: _____

4. Use the next two pages for prewriting!

Take a moment to select and organize (and even add to) the parts of your prewriting that you feel best support your purpose.

Now it's time to write. Remember that you can use the prewriting work on these pages as a guide, but if you feel inspired to go in a different direction while you're writing, go for it!

Story Title:

```

```

_____

_____

_____

_____

_____

_____

_____

_____

_____

_____

_____

_____

_____

_____

_____

_____

_____

_____

Writing Exercise #13

1. Underline your choice of prompt:
   a. Lollipop probability machine
   b. If someone gave you $1,000,000 but said you had to spend it all in one day, what would you spend it on?

2. Determine a purpose for your writing: _____

3. Select an appropriate prewriting exercise: _____

4. Use the next two pages for prewriting!

Take a moment to select and organize (and even add to) the parts of your prewriting that you feel best support your purpose.

Now it's time to write. Remember that you can use the prewriting work on these pages as a guide, but if you feel inspired to go in a different direction while you're writing, go for it!

Story Title:

_____

Writing Exercise #14

1. Underline your choice of prompt:
   a. **When was a time that you felt excluded from something you really wanted to be part of?**
   b. **Fudge popsicle in winter**

2. Determine a purpose for your writing: _____

3. Select an appropriate prewriting exercise: _____

4. Use the next two pages for prewriting!

Take a moment to select and organize (and even add to) the parts of your prewriting that you feel best support your purpose.

Now it's time to write. Remember that you can use the prewriting work on these pages as a guide, but if you feel inspired to go in a different direction while you're writing, go for it!

Story Title:

Writing Exercise #15

1. Underline your choice of prompt:
   a. What makes someone popular in school? What *should*?
   b. If you could travel back in time but only *observe* the world around you, where and when would you go? Why?

2. Determine a purpose for your writing: _____

3. Select an appropriate prewriting exercise: _____

4. Use the next two pages for prewriting!

Take a moment to select and organize (and even add to) the parts of your prewriting that you feel best support your purpose.

Now it's time to write. Remember that you can use the prewriting work on these pages as a guide, but if you feel inspired to go in a different direction while you're writing, go for it!

Story Title: